HOW TO SURVIVE YOUR PARENTS' DIVORCE

Also by Nancy O'Keefe Bolick

Shaker Inventions

Shaker Villages

HOW TO
SURVIVE
YOUR
PARENTS'
DIVORCE

by NANCY O'KEEFE BOLICK

The Changing Family
Franklin Watts
New York   Chicago   London   Toronto   Sydney

To Doug, Katie, and Christopher, lucky in love and family.

And to every kid who suffers the pain and fear of divorce. Thanks to those of you who shared your stories.

Library of Congress Cataloging-in-Publication Data

Bolick, Nancy O'Keefe.
How to survive your parents' divorce / by Nancy O'Keefe Bolick.
p.   cm. — (The Changing family)
Includes index.
ISBN 0-531-11054-0 (lib. bdg.)
1. Children of divorced parents—Juvenile literature.   2. Divorce—
Juvenile literature.   I. Title.   II. Series: Changing family (New
York, N.Y.)
HQ777.5.B647   1994
306.89—dc20
94-15075   CIP   AC

CONTENTS

ACKNOWLEDGMENTS

I wish it weren't necessary to write a book about how to survive your parents' divorce. Kids don't cause divorce and they're affected by it more than anyone else. It is almost always a traumatic experience.

The kids who agreed to talk with me about their families are brave and admirable people. It was often hard for them to reveal their feelings and admit their pain, but they did it. They did it so that other kids going through the same things could learn a little from their painful experiences. They hope it will help.

Many people gave me their time and expertise. I particularly want to thank Kathryn O'Keefe, Steve Mueller, Clara Fulton, Lynne Jordan, Susan and Walter DeMelle, and Thomas May for putting me in touch with kids. I thank Barry Lewis, Dave Brewer, Frances Goldfield, Robin Deutsch, Bob Scott, and Michael Nesson for giving me a broader look at divorce.

For their creative input and keen eyes, I thank Doug Bolick, Katie Bolick, and Kevin O'Keefe—and for moral support, Chet Arnold.

INTRODUCTION

A few years ago, when asked if I would write a book about how kids survive divorce, I said it sounded like an interesting project and I'd like to think about it. I'd been married for a long time at that point, and my two children were teenagers. My husband and I had plenty of friends who were divorced, and our children knew lots of kids whose parents had split up. I knew it was hardly ever an easy thing for families.

I decided to take on the project because I thought if kids had the chance to hear from others who had experienced divorce, it might help them navigate the same tough terrain should their turn come. Misery loves company, but it also needs to believe there's hope that things might eventually get a little easier. If there were kids out there willing to describe what divorce was like for them, and share the ways they handled it, then it was worth listening to them.

In the next two years I interviewed young people from the ages of thirteen to twenty-two. I found them in Massachusetts, where I live, and in Connecticut, Ohio, South Dakota, and Florida. They were willing to meet with me and tell me their stories because they had learned that talking about their anger, fears, and hopes had helped. Many had shared their feelings with therapists and school guidance counselors and with their peers in divorce support groups.

Some kids approached counselors and groups willingly, and others had to be cajoled. But once they took that first step, almost all of them said they were glad they'd made contact. The counselors were able to get them talking about their pain. And the kids in the groups realized they weren't alone. The groups became a safe place where they could meet others who were dealing with the same issues; a place where it was okay to say how hard life during and after divorce had become. All of that helped.

You may not be lucky enough to have a guidance counselor you can share your feelings with. Chances are there's no divorce support group in your school, because I found they were rare. But you've opened this book, and you're about to read about other kids just like you. They've been lucky because they were able to start talking.

Maybe you will be lucky too, after you have read the descriptions of their feelings.

It's sad but true: finding young people to interview for a book about divorce was the easiest part of this project. Half of all marriages eventually fall apart; over a million American children are left in the wake of divorce every year.

Even though family breakups are all too familiar, every individual family is different, and so is every divorce. But in some larger ways, families share more similarities than differences when it comes to divorce, because no matter what the individual circumstances, change and loss are part of the mix. Those are hard things for most people to handle.

When a man and a woman who have married and had children decide— for whatever reason—that they can't live together anymore, everyone involved loses something. Parents lose their partners, their sense of identity, their future as part of a team, and their dreams. And they lose the connection they had to their children before the divorce. The children will end up living with one parent, usually the mother, or perhaps go to live with other family members. Whatever the arrangement, one person becomes a single parent with day-to-day parental responsibilities and the other becomes a parent who no longer lives at home. The former roles of mother and father can't help but be different.

Almost all the kids I interviewed said they blamed themselves for their parents' divorce at some point. But as one psychologist who works with families told me, children don't cause divorce. They're generally a great source of joy for parents, but they can add stress to a troubled marriage. Yet managing stress is a task of being an adult. When parents fail at that, it's not the kids' fault.

So never think that divorce is the kids' problem. And don't let adults who aren't healthy enough to manage stress try to blame you for it. It's important for you to remember that what caused your parents' divorce is between them. What you did or didn't do wasn't a factor.

But divorce has turned your world upside down. It's becoming clear to people who study families of divorce that children are often the biggest losers when parents split up. Some of them suffer more, and longer, than their parents. They lose the sense of protection a family is supposed to provide, the sheltering umbrella under which they can develop and mature. They lose the day-to-day presence of either their mother or father and the guidance and support of the parent who isn't living at home anymore. They lose trust in their parents, in other people, in themselves, and in the future.

Kids don't always know the rules of recovering from divorce, either. Not many people do. Too often, kids have to learn new ways of coping with all of this loss on their own, while their parents keep on slugging it out and while other people in their lives—family, friends, teachers, and guidance counselors—fumble about trying to help them. Far too often, they become pawns in the games their mothers and fathers play to hurt each other after they separate.

Some children have a very hard time. They become depressed and draw away from their friends. With family problems always on their minds, they become distracted and get into trouble at school. At the least, their grades slide downhill, and at the worst, they become discipline problems, regular visitors to the principal's office. They may be attracted to all the things just waiting to trip adolescents up: drugs, alcohol, sex. They might succumb to all of these things some of the time, or one of them all the time. For them, moving on to life after divorce is hard.

Other kids are more fortunate. Perhaps their personalities are optimistic by nature, making it easier to cope. Maybe their parents bend over backwards to be civil to each other and to help their children through the tough times. Maybe the kids are able to let people who care guide them through the rough spots. Maybe they're just people who can bounce back from life's blows without knowing quite how they do it.

But even the lucky ones are wounded by divorce, and the hurt can last a long time. At some level in their psyches, most of the kids I interviewed felt betrayed by their parents, the people who were supposed to take care of them. They may believe they're better off without their parents' fighting, and may be glad to live without the constant tension of unhappy homes. But it's still not the way they thought their families were supposed to behave.

Just how do kids see life when a family splits apart at the seams? Armed with a tape recorder and notebook, I interviewed junior and senior high school students in many places. Guidance counselors and school principals led me to kids who were dealing with divorce. I met the young people in counselors' offices, in libraries, and in cafeterias, and spent time talking with each one. I followed up some of these interviews with conversations on the phone.

Every student got permission from at least one parent to talk with me. I assured them that I'd protect their privacy by not using their real names or revealing where they lived. I thank them all for speaking out.

Still, our meetings were short, jammed into free periods or lunch breaks, and I had no ongoing relationship with any of the people I interviewed. They were brave to share so much with a stranger. But I know they couldn't tell me all the things they might tell a counselor they knew well and trusted more. I suspect they all have fears and memories they keep buried, sometimes even from themselves.

Despite their candor, I suspect many of them were trying to protect themselves by keeping some part of their feelings private. Who wants to share the details of loneliness and fear and despair? Why broadcast the tears in the night, or the hate they must sometimes feel for their parents, or confront fears about the future?

What you're about to read isn't the result of a scientific study. I didn't choose kids to interview on the basis of how well or poorly they were doing, or how articulate they were, or how cooperative they'd been with counselors. I didn't develop a formula about the timing of the divorce or the particular circumstances surrounding it. All I wanted was to talk to kids who'd been through it.

I interviewed about two dozen young people in the course of my research. All of their stories were different—and similar. I picked eleven of them to describe in detail to illustrate all of the ramifications of divorce. It's their voices you will hear in this book.

CHAPTER ONE

ROB:
LOSING HIS CHILDHOOD
TO DIVORCE

You'd never guess from looking at Rob that he carries burdens much heavier than his fourteen years should have to shoulder. An eighth-grader in a suburb of Hartford, Connecticut, Rob is cute, upbeat, and articulate. He's into sports and fitness, and he has lots of friends. He's a take-charge kind of guy and if you met him you'd think he was a typical all-American boy.

Rob *is* typical, but not in the way he appears. Like so many American kids in the 1990s, he's been robbed of the carefree ease of childhood. His father took off when Rob was in the sixth grade, leaving him, his younger sister, and their mother to regroup and forge a new kind of family. Rob has emerged as the surrogate head of the household, looking out for his mother and his sister, assuming many of the duties of his father. He says he's managing everything just fine, thank you, but you can't help but think he's been served too full a plate at the age of fourteen.

Maybe he's just an optimist by nature, but Rob

talks a good game. He's self-confident and smiling when we meet in a small conference room in his junior high school, and he's so willing to discuss his parents' divorce that he skips a class later so he can sit in on my interview with his classmate, Suzanne. This is the kind of boy mothers love to have their kids hang out with—a cheerful, vibrant guy who played on a championship soccer team before he switched to football this year, who looks out for his younger sister, who's a leader in his class. Rob, who acts as though he knows what's going on, is in a bit of a hurry to grow up, and can't wait to turn sixteen so he can start driving.

Rob does a great job of covering over the hurt of the divorce. He sounds so rational for an adolescent, so full of ways of dealing with a tough situation, but hints of anger and bitterness still manage to creep out from behind the happy front he wears, and you wonder how he handles these emotions when he's alone.

Here's Rob sounding brave:

"I used to worry about my parents getting divorced, but then when it happened, I thought it was going to be so much worse than it really was. I realized it was better because Mom and Dad didn't fight, Dad didn't yell at me or at Mom or my sister, and he was out of the house. My dad's the one who's losing in the long run."

But then listen to him as he remembers the day his father moved out.

"I was twelve, and one night I was walking through the kitchen. Mom and Dad were ar-

guing over money and I just thought something
was up. I got out of the way and went to bed.
The next morning when I woke up, my mother
called my sister and me. 'Come here you two,
I have something to tell you,' she said. 'Your
dad left last night and he and I have decided to
get a divorce.'

"I said, 'Where's Dad now?' And Mom told
us he was staying at our grandmother's.

"My sister started crying, but I didn't. I
was mad, but I didn't cry. I went into my room
and punched the nearest thing, which was the
window. My hand went right through it. The
only time I saw my dad for the next month was
when he came over to fix that window."

Rob has taken sides in the family feud and now
relishes his roles as his mother's confidante and his
sister's protector. They're roles he takes on with his
friends, too.

"I can talk to my mom about everything. I
don't talk to my dad about anything, even school.
He doesn't care about me. One time I got two Bs
on my report card and when I told him he said,
'Yeah?' I said, 'Okay, I guess you don't want to
see the rest of it. That's okay with me.'

"My dad's an electrician, and I know he
used to drink on the job when he was living with
us. He'd come home from work and just sit like
a lump in front of the TV. I'd say 'How was
your day?' and he'd say 'fine' and that would
be it.

"My mom would go to bed after a while, or he'd go first. They never went at the same time. We never did things together. Once in a while he'd take me out on a side job with him, but that was about it.

"I never made the effort to do things with him and I'm glad I didn't because if we had done a lot together, and then he left, it would have torn me apart. As it is, it doesn't hurt me.

"I only spend a few hours a month with him now, but I still get mad when he's a jerk to my mom and I don't really want to do anything with him. Last summer he invited me to the beach with him but I wouldn't go. My sister did, but I went with a friend instead."

Rob knows what he's missing in his father and admits he makes little effort to establish a relationship with him. He's decided that instead of wishing for what he never had, he'll put his energy into what he does have—his mother and sister.

"It was bad with my dad around before the divorce, but I never said anything to Mom. I didn't want to hurt her feelings. I told her after-wards how I felt and she said she suspected that's the way it was. He's not a good father. He doesn't know how to care for kids. He watches sports on TV, drinks beer, and goes out with the boys. That's about it."

Rob dismisses his father's way of life like some parents shrug their shoulders in frustration with kids who won't toe the line. If his father won't do what he's supposed to do, then Rob will take up the slack at home.

"Before the divorce my mom used to work part-time and my dad worked longer hours. She'd get home early and when we got home from school the whole house would be picked up. Now she's working full-time for the government in Hartford and she can't do all she used to. I do a lot of things without her asking me to. I take out the trash, fix things, do dishes, wash floors, all the everyday things Mom can't do. I don't mind. The house gets messy and someone has to pick it up."

Rob sounds more mature than fourteen when he talks about his twelve-year-old sister. He sounds like a dad.

"Sometimes I fight with her over stupid things. Girls take things harder than boys, and she's at a tough age. I'll ask her to pick up and she'll say no. I'll get mad and just do it myself.

"But she's a good kid, and the divorce has been hard on her. I watch out for her in school. She tells me the boys she likes and I'll tell her about who's okay and who isn't. I'm civilized," he says. *"I'll be fifteen in June."*

In his mind, and maybe his mother's, Rob's reacting in a mature and positive way to divorce. He's assumed adult responsibilities at the age of fourteen and doing a pretty good job of it. But is Rob walking through life before he's learned to crawl? At his age it's normal for boys to begin to create distance between themselves and their mothers. At his age a boy needs the strong presence of a father to guide him towards manhood. But the divorce has forced Rob to form a stronger bond with his mother and to dismiss his father. He's much more aware of his mother's feelings than he would have to be if his father were around, and all too aware of his father's shortcomings.

"I hate to say it, but I really feel differently about my parents. I love my mom. She treats me wicked good. I just like my dad. Sometimes he tries to compete with Mom. But she's just so much more caring than he is," Rob says.

Rob also looks out for his mother's emotional life in a way he wouldn't need to if his family was intact.

"Mom was never happy with Dad. I'm glad he left because now she has a boyfriend and she's happy."

His mother's boyfriend is the father of Rob's good friend Eddie.

"They met because Eddie and I both play football," Rob explains.

"Eddie's parents are divorced, and his mom is like my dad. But his dad is a cool guy. He likes kids. He takes us to ball games and does a lot of stuff with us. He and my mom get along because they treat kids the same way. I'd like it if they got married, but they aren't talking about that yet."

Time will tell how Rob's early burdens will affect him. If he has his way, he says, it won't hold him back from approaching marriage and a family of his own, from assuming adult responsibilities he knows only too well belong to fathers. For now, he tries to talk about his situation and do the best with what he's been dealt. That's one part of the advice he offers for young boys going through the same thing.

"If you have a close friend, talk to him. It's a good idea to talk to kids your age or kids just a bit older about your life, whether they're from divorced families or not. I can tell my friend Eddie just about anything, and that seems to help," he says.

Rob also advises trying to find out what went wrong in your parents' marriage so you won't feel responsible for what happened. He's lucky that he can really talk with his mother.

"I really wanted to find out what happened. I talk to Mom and Dad, and by me finding out, I didn't think it was my fault. Just ask them: 'Why did you separate?' If they tell you, you feel a lot better inside. You can say, 'Well, it wasn't me. It didn't have anything to do with me.' "

The football field is his other outlet.

"Sports are an excellent way to cope. I used to play soccer but I always felt frustrated after a game. Then I went out for football.
"I'd tell boys, go for football if your parents

let you. I never come off the field with one worry in the world. It's a game that lets you take so much anger out, unlike soccer, where there are more restrictions.

"It may sound brutal, but even if you're a small guy you can crack kids on the football field and that feels great. It calms you down, makes you feel so much better. Even my mom has seen how football has changed me."

Sometimes reading *Sports Illustrated* helps Rob, too. His sister handles things, he says, by going for walks, running, and riding her bike.

"Just find something that will take your mind off it, and do that. Do whatever works," says Rob.

The teachers and counselors at Rob's school know what he's dealing with. They say he's smart but often he's not too motivated. He can be moody. They say he clashes with teachers who try to push him to the limits of his ability. He needs structure from other adults, they say, but he fights it because he wants to be in control. He's found success doing that at home.

They also recognize that Rob is a natural leader, a kid who looks out for other kids smaller and less popular than he is, who is always fair in his dealings with everyone. He's learned to be that way at home, too.

Rob's doing okay, but he's still angry. He needs to be in charge. If he can work through those things he'll have a much better chance of finding the happy, stable marriage he wants for himself later on.

CHAPTER TWO

ANTHONY: DIVORCE, DIVORCE, AND MORE DIVORCE

I didn't ask Anthony if he'd ever tried to draw his family tree. But if he were to attempt it, the tangled limbs would branch out in so many directions, and so many birds would perch on them, that it would be impossible to decipher the lines connecting mother and father, sister and brother, husband and wife.

Anthony is only nineteen, but he's survived three fathers, two mothers, and three divorces so far in his short life. The only constant has been his birth mother, with whom he's always lived. He was about seven at the time of the first divorce, and at the time we met, his mother's second marriage had just broken up. His father had remarried and divorced again, too. And the summer before, when he was eighteen, Anthony met a man he never even knew existed—his biological father. His mother had kept him a secret all these years.

Anthony is a senior at a Florida high school, a sprawling suburban complex dotted with palm trees and walking paths. There's a huge outdoor swimming pool on campus and the security guards scoot around on golf carts from building to building. Anthony, a tall, muscular, handsome young man in shorts and a tank top, looks at home in the mellow sunshine that kisses his school. I'm not surprised when he says he's a surfer, and that he spends a lot of time at the beach. Just looking at him you'd think he had it made.

But talking with Anthony makes you realize he hasn't had an easy ride. The Florida sunshine and the swaying coconut palms form a seductive cover for a family life that has been anything but comfortable. Anthony has had to absorb a lot of losses in his time. Still, he talks freely about his home life. He has ambitions, and he's determined to form a better future than the tumultuous past that defined his childhood and adolescence.

When Anthony tries to assign blame for some of the chaos, he targets himself, his parents, and his stepparents. ''I was only seven or eight at the time of the first divorce, so I didn't really know what was going on. You don't understand when you're a little kid. But I knew my dad was having an affair with another woman, and I blamed him for that.

''My mom remarried about five years ago and she and my stepfather just split up a few months ago. Money was an issue with them, and I blame both of them for not being rational and talking their problems out. Money shouldn't lead to divorce.

''But I may have played a part, too. I'd get

into arguments with Paul, my stepfather, and then my mom would get dragged in and then they'd get to arguing. When that happened I'd feel like I was the whole problem, which I kind of guess I was. I think kids can be a reason parents fight, especially in stepfamilies."

Anthony may be right when he says parents get dragged into arguments between children and stepparents. But he's wrong to think that when kids start the arguments they're contributing to the divorce. Managing family fights is still a responsibility that parents, not children, must assume.

"I was about thirteen or fourteen when my mother remarried, and I rebelled when my stepfather tried to give me orders. He'd say 'Go clean your room' and I'd come back with 'No. You're not my father.'

"Kids that age are always telling their stepparent terrible things over and over. 'You're not my daddy. Get out of here. I won't listen to you because you aren't my real dad.' Stuff like that. It's not fair, because here's a guy just coming into the family and he doesn't know all the ropes yet. He's trying to do his best, but you think he's a total butthead.

"So he's doing the best he can and then he hears someone he's helping to feed and clothe say all that stuff, and I'm sure it crushes the guy. Money and kids—the two leading causes of divorce."

Anthony wonders if his mother's second marriage would have survived if he had behaved differently. "If I could go back to when they were first married and I was in that rebellious stage against my stepfather, I'd be more than happy to change it. Now I realize how silly a game that is."

Anthony's family was living in Alabama at the time of the first divorce, and it was then that he and his brother had to make the most crucial decision a seven-year-old could be called on to make: Which parent do you want to live with?

"At the divorce trial the judge took me and my brother aside in a small room and asked us which of our parents we wanted to live with. That was one of the hardest decisions I've ever had to make. I had mixed emotions. I kind of understood what my dad did wrong to my mom—he was having an affair with her best friend. But I couldn't cope with deciding which one I was going to stay with. Everything was going through my mind at once. What do I do? Where will I go? Where will I end up?

"I thought about whether things would be the same or not. Should I go with Mom or Dad? He beat me sometimes and I didn't like that, and all he wanted to do was drink beer and party. My brother and I decided Mom was the better one for us to grow up with. She never raised a hand to us and was always more of a provider. My brother and I were unanimous in *that decision, although we've never talked about it since then.*

"Things changed after that. My dad was in the Army and Mom was working. But she had to work more after the divorce and money was a problem. Before, if I asked for toys or candy, they'd buy them for me. After, Mom would apologize and say money was tight.

"While we were in Alabama and my father was in the Army, we saw him every weekend. Sometimes it was okay, and sometimes it wasn't. He was living with the woman he had the affair with and her daughters, who were about my age. My brother and I would go over to stay with them, and we'd end up having to do yard work while the girls sat back on the couch. Dad eventually married her, but now they're getting divorced, too.

"Actually, I've only seen my dad twice in the past seven years, and I don't remember all that much about him. I know he drinks, and I remember him as always having a beer in his hands. Once when we visited him, when we were still little kids, he gave us beer and pot."

Although he didn't spend much time with his father, Anthony remembers the violence. "He'd give me a pretty good whipping if I didn't get a good report card or if I flipped someone off. It wasn't major league beating, but it felt like it when I was a little kid. When a guy's six foot something and you're just three feet tall, it's scary."

After his mother moved the family to Florida, Anthony and his brother had only occasional contact with their father.

"Once he came to town and took us to lunch, but we didn't know what to talk about. He'd sent one card and one small gift in the previous seven years. We'd write notes to him but he'd never answer them."

Anthony talks about his attempts to stay in touch with his father in a calm way, but later, explaining how things are now between him and Paul, his stepfather, his eyes blaze with bitter memories of the first divorce.

"When I said good-bye to my stepfather, I gave him the biggest hug of my life. I wanted to cry but I didn't—that's sissy stuff. Paul sat me and my brother down and we talked about what was happening. He told us he loved us and that the divorce was nowhere near being our fault, that he'd always be there if we needed him. If he wants to stay in touch, I'll be more than happy to.

"But I'm not going to fall for the same thing that I did with the last guy. I wrote him ten million times and got one card back. I wrote till my hand almost fell off. He still doesn't call or write. We could be dead and he wouldn't know it."

And then Anthony throws a bombshell into the conversation.

"He's not my real dad anyway. I just met the real one last summer. My mom took us to Chicago to meet him and tried to explain that they loved each other a lot but that she was only eighteen when she got pregnant with me. She dropped out of school to have me, but she just wasn't ready for marriage.

"Mom had been sending him notes and pictures of me all along, but I never knew. When she told me, I was shocked and mad that I was just now finding this out. When we met for dinner, we had an awkward time without much conversation, and then we took pictures so we could remember each other. He has three daughters now that I've never met."

Three fathers in nineteen years adds up to a lot of loss for Anthony. Still, he tries to sound casual about his stepfather, who moved to a different part of the state after the divorce.

"In a way it didn't hit me as hard as the first time, when I was a little kid, because I've been through it. But then it hit me very hard, because Paul was more of a father to me than the other guy ever was. He'd take us outside to play catch, out on boats, and to football games, those father-son kinds of activities. I could talk to him about girl problems, or drugs. I was with him for five years, so I guess I learned to love him.

"Paul's already sent us more money and cards at Christmas and birthdays than my first

father ever did. He says we can come to visit him anytime, and he'll always be there if we need him. I don't know if that will work out, but we can always call him on the phone.''

Although he wishes this second marriage had flourished, Anthony is realistic and knows there are things about it he won't miss.

''The good part is now I won't have to listen to arguments in the middle of the night. My mom and Paul could be the most loving couple in the world sometimes and the most hating at other times. Usually they fought at night, and usually it was over money. I'd put a pillow over my head or turn the radio up and close the door so I wouldn't hear them.

''A couple of times I thought I should try to talk with them about it, but I didn't think it was my place to interfere with what they were going through. The few times I did try to talk with my mom about it, sometimes she'd give me an answer and sometimes she wouldn't. It's a touchy subject why parents, or couples, argue. I know that when I argue with my girlfriend, I don't want to talk about it.

''When they decided to separate, Mom sat my brother and me down and told us what they were doing, and when they finally decided to divorce, she did the same thing. I asked her why and she didn't say much, just went up to her room and cried.

"It all went back to money issues. Paul just didn't make that much. Mom worked harder and made more than he did. We always had food in the fridge, and after work Mom would come home, cook dinner, clean the house. Paul did the laundry and cleaned, too. He just felt he needed more money for household bills, and she wanted to keep more of her salary.

"In a way I think maybe they should have sat down and talked rationally instead of sepa-rating. I think there was a lot of selfishness on both their parts. I vow that money isn't going to come between me and my family when I get married."

It's not surprising that Anthony says he'd like to have plenty of money when he's on his own.

"But I won't let it get in the way of me and my wife and my family, because I don't want my kids to go through the same things I did when I was a kid. I'd avoid trouble by doing my best to give my wife whatever she needed. If she made more money than I did, I'd tell her she should keep some for herself."

With his record of disappointments, I wonder if Anthony worries about being able to trust people. It would be hard to blame him if he didn't.

"Yes, I think I can be a trusting person," he says. *"As long as you respect and trust me,*

I'll respect and trust you back. That's the way it is with my girlfriend and me.

"And I trust my mom. My life hasn't been as hard as others. My mom's raised me all my life and kind of spoiled me. I think my life has gone pretty well, even with having only one parent most of the time."

Anthony dreams of a future as a chef, a paramedic, a police officer, maybe as a military man. "I've changed my mind ten million times," he says. He wants to go to college, get married, and do all the things with his kids that he wishes his father had done with him.

He's different from the man he thought was his birth father in another way, too. He blames many of his father's problems on alcohol and has decided that it won't play a big role in his life. Anthony drinks occasionally at parties, but prefers to be the designated driver home. Yet his brother, raised in the same circumstances, hasn't fared as well.

"He's already gotten into trouble, and he won't go to college," says Anthony.

Anthony faults his mother and stepfather for fighting and has some advice for kids caught in the cross fire at home.

"For some kids—the real sensitive kind who don't like to hear parents argue—the best thing is to leave the house. Most of the time I'm like that, sensitive, although I try to act tough

around my friends. I'd usually go out to the beach, paddle out to catch a few waves and get my mind back together. Or I'd go to my girlfriend's house because she listens to me and comforts me. I started going out with her when the divorce happened.

"I think parents' arguing is something a son or a daughter shouldn't have to hear. I never liked it, either the first time or the second. Parents should argue quietly and rationally or out of the kids' hearing.

"I play football and rugby and I wrestle, and sometimes when I'm mad, I take my anger out on the opposing team. I get all fired up, and in a way that makes me compete better. But in another way you're all confused and you haven't got your mind together, and that's hard. When I feel confused like that, that's when I hate my mom and stepfather because of the fighting."

Having a girlfriend has been a good thing for Anthony.

"We don't fight, and she's been a real help to me through the divorce. She really listens."

Anthony cares about his girlfriend a great deal, but he hangs back from making a commitment to her at this time. That reluctance may stem from his experience with loss. Or it may be a mature reaction, a recognition that he has too much to do before he settles down.

"I haven't told her I love her yet, even though I feel it. I just can't build up the nerve to say anything like that." Marriage, Anthony says, will have to wait until he's finished with college and in a position to provide for a family.

CHAPTER THREE

KRISTI:
FIGHTING THE ISOLATION

"I'm not like everyone else and I don't want to be,"

says Kristi with a hint of defiance in her voice. She's thirteen, an eighth-grader in a suburban Connecticut junior high.

"I think that being from a divorced family has something to do with that."

Kristi tucks her long hair behind her ears and perches at the edge of a chair as she talks with me in her school guidance counselor's office. A thoughtful and articulate girl dressed in jeans and a big sweater, she looks like a million other kids navigating the rocky terrain of early adolescence and seems to be doing it fairly well.

But what you see with Kristi isn't what you get when she begins to talk about herself. An only child, she was five when her parents divorced, and she's candid about the scars that remain, which she attributes to her family's breakup.

Eight years after the fact, Kristi sounds disgusted with parents who still fight and put her in the middle of their arguments. She thinks her friends from intact families are living in a dreamworld and resents them for being smug. She totes up her losses and struggles to carve a safe place for herself in the world. But she says that's hard to do.

> *"I want to have my childhood like everyone else does,"* says Kristi, who clearly thinks she's missed out on years of innocence and security that she sees her friends taking for granted.

> *"Kids in perfect little families don't have any clue about what it's like to go through a divorce. They think you eventually just forget about it, but you don't. You can't. It's in the back of your mind every single day,"* she says.

Being thirteen and in the eighth grade is tough enough without adding divorce to the things kids worry about every day. No matter how much they wish it didn't matter, most of them spend a lot of time and energy trying to figure out where they stand with the people they want as friends. Being like everyone else is all that counts. Kids of divorced parents, like Kristi, often feel different from everyone else, which is just about the last thing they need.

Although it seems as though divorce is so common that nobody thinks twice about it these days, Kristi sees herself as different from the girls she knows who have never had to deal with it. Without realizing what they're doing, they make assumptions and say things that hurt her deeply. When that happens, it just reinforces the distance she believes divorce has created between her and other people.

Kristi's been very upset about thoughtless comments from her friends, but she's able to use her journal as a way to channel that hurt into self-awareness. Writing lets her open up in a way she finds hard to do face-to-face. One thoughtless comment really got her going and she vented her feelings on paper.

"Our parents are all settled down and stuff. That one phrase really set me off and it was what my supposed-to-be best friend said to me," Kristi wrote in one entry.

"A bunch of us were just sitting around when she said that to me. My response was, 'It's not my fault my parents are divorced. You don't know what it feels like and you couldn't care less!' I started to cry; that one sentence hurt me so much that nobody could ever imagine so much pain.

"My friend knows my mom goes out with guys and I guess she thinks that's weird. She's always asking my mom questions that are none of her business, about her dates and where she's going. I admit that sometimes it's embarrassing when my mom has a boyfriend and I wonder what they're doing. But she can take care of herself.

"My friend hasn't a clue about my life be-

cause her life is a fairy tale. Her parents never fight around her so she's got this idea that if your parents aren't married, they aren't normal. She should open up her eyes and see that most of today's society is made up of divorced parents.''

There have been other times Kristi's situation has made her feel estranged. "In third grade I made my first communion, but the priest said my parents couldn't take communion because they were divorced. I heard that and it made me feel odd.''

Although she was very young, Kristi remembers distinctly the night everything fell apart between her parents. It has become a canyon dividing her life into "before" and "after" segments that she thinks will never be bridged.

> *"My mom and I were going over to a neighbor's house and my dad called Mom back in. She told me to stay right where I was, so I waited for her outside. Then I heard them both screaming at each other and I went in and watched. I saw them fighting, hitting each other, and it felt like my world was tearing apart. My mom and I spent that night at our neighbor's house. Later, I went to my grandfather's for a few weeks while they sorted things out.''*

She was only five, but somehow, the family split didn't surprise Kristi.

*"I don't have any happy memories of my
parents together. Most of my memories are of
them fighting over something. But I wasn't
afraid of them. I thought they'd probably get a
divorce even though I didn't know what divorce
meant. I just knew something bad was going to
happen."*

Even so, like many kids, Kristi has wrestled with
her role in the divorce.

*"I felt it was my fault when it happened,
that I'd done something wrong that made them
hate me. But I talked about that recently with
them and I know it wasn't my fault, that they
were two different people after they had me.
They both loved me, but they changed.*

*"My dad said that before I came my mom
was easygoing. Now she's a perfectionist. Dad
was the same after they had me but I guess Mom
wanted him to change. Finally, I'm beginning
to understand that they got divorced because
they just couldn't stay together anymore."*

Kristi has lived with her mother since the divorce.
Her father has remarried, but even though he has a
new wife and a baby daughter, he and Kristi's mother
continue the feud that's been near the boiling point ever
since they broke up. Kristi resents being in the middle
of it.

*"I'm the referee in my parents' fights. They
argue about if Dad got the check to her on time,*

*or if he isn't paying my medical bills, or if Mom
didn't do this or that.*

*"They don't give me a chance to decide
what I think about them for myself. They don't
like each other and I know they're never going
to like each other. They can hardly stay in the
same room. Mom says mean things about Dad.
She calls him a jerk, tells me he never does
anything for me, and when I question her about
that she says I should ask him for myself. She
doesn't realize that hurts me."*

Kristi knows her parents use her as a Ping-Pong
ball in a hate game they don't seem to know how to
stop. She resents being forced to take sides, and she
won't do it.

*"I like them equally. They're my mother
and father. I try to keep them in line so they
don't fight so much. I wish they could just get
along."*

One of the consequences of her parents' divorce
and their continued squabbling since is Kristi's reluctance to confide in them, and to open herself up to
others.

*"I'm not open with my parents. If my mom
wants to get the answer to even a simple question out of me, she has to pry. I don't want to
talk because I'm afraid she'll hurt me somehow.
I don't want to be hurt again. I can talk with
my dad better, but I only see him every other*

weekend. And now he has a new family, and there are things I find it hard to bring up with him.

"For example, I don't think my stepmother really trusts me. She was nice before they got married, and we used to go places together. But since she had the baby—my half sister— she's changed. The baby's the center of their world now, and I don't get much attention when I'm at their house. I thought about talking with my dad about it, but I really don't want to bring it up. I'm afraid that if I do, something will happen to them and that will be just another family splitting up."

It sounds as if Kristi's fears of yet another family falling apart are so great that she's unwilling to risk any openness with either of her parents. Yet getting her concerns out in the open would help them understand what she's thinking and give them a chance to put her fears into context.

On the one hand, Kristi explains her life easily and describes herself as outgoing, the kind of person who'll talk to anyone. On the other hand, she admits she won't share deep feelings with people she doesn't know, or get close to people she suspects won't be a permanent part of her life. The inner and outer Kristi don't match up.

"When I make friends, I'm careful not to let them know everything about me. I guess that's because everyone and everything I've

ever loved has died. My grandfather died. My cat, who I could kind of talk to and feel he understood, died. And my dog died.

"I make it a point not to get too close to the men my mom goes out with. Most of them have been really nice, but when they stopped seeing each other I really didn't notice, because I wasn't attached. I'd talk, let them get to know me a little, but I never wanted them to get to know me really well. If you keep everything inside, no one's going to hurt you."

The problem for her, Kristi says, is a wound so deep she hasn't found a way to bandage it over very quickly.

"You feel like your parents are betraying you when they get divorced. You don't want to trust them again because you had all your trust in them and they just go and break up. You're left in the middle between them and you feel nobody loves you."

Although she's only thirteen and has a long time to go before she considers marriage for herself, when Kristi thinks about the future, she's cautious. "When I have my own family, I want to really make sure I love the person and he loves me and we get along before we have kids, because I don't think any kid should have to go through a divorce.

"If things got rocky, I'd discuss it with my husband and kids so they'd understand what was happening. It's not fair to use kids as a

barrier. But it's not good for parents to stay together if love has died. Kids feel they aren't loved then, either. I think parents have to talk with their kids, and if the unhappiness is ruining everyone's lives, then get a divorce.

"I know love dies. But I think a lot of parents get divorced too fast. They should really go over everything, what they actually think, for a few months. Parents are more involved in hurting each other than in what their kids are feeling. They don't remember what it's like to be a kid. They've got to try to figure out what they want without so much anger. They should involve kids so they understand, but not so much that it becomes the kids' problems."

Assuming her parents' problems is a heavy load on Kristi, as it is for so many kids of divorce. She wants to stay close to her dad but knows that when she gets to high school, she'll probably want to stay at home with her friends on the weekends rather than go to his house in a neighboring town. When she sees him now, she wants to be friendly with her stepmother, but she feels guilty about leaving her real mother alone. She likes her little stepsister, but admits she herself needs attention, too. She wants her mother to be happy, but can't trust herself to get close to her mother's men friends.

Kristi is beginning to meet kids who've been through divorce, and as she gets to know them better, she finds it easier to talk about her own situation. "My best friend now is my boyfriend, Jesse. We talk about our parents and divorce and we help each other. His mom is remarried and heading for her second divorce, and he's gone back and forth between his mom and his dad. He's trying to help them with options, whether to move to a cheaper place or stay here. I don't think he should have to be involved in that. The adults should work it out themselves," she says.

As she matures, Kristi is learning ways to deal with her sadness, with the feelings that she's so different and isolated from everyone else. One of the best things she's done for herself is to start taking a chance on communicating more with her parents.

> *"I think you've got to talk. Get it all out. Even better is to write about it, because if it's on paper they can understand better. I can talk to my dad, but my way of communicating with my mother is by writing stories. I just start writing, get all my feelings out, every single one—who I'm angry at, why I am, if I can trust them again, things like that. It helps her understand me."*

But acknowledging that talking it out is the fastest way to healing is one thing. Actually doing it is another for many people. Kristi writes a lot, putting some distance between herself and her mother, and that helps her be more frank.

> *"Kids who just can't talk may have better luck with other things," she says. "Maybe they can meditate, get in touch with where they are*

right now. Or go for a walk, do something. I like to walk in the woods near my house. It's peaceful there. It's my place, and no one can hurt me. Everyone has to find his own safe place.''

CHAPTER FOUR

CURTIS: TRYING TO LET GO OF THE ANGER

If rage could generate electricity, then Curtis had enough energy bottled inside to light up Boston's Fenway Park for a night baseball game when we first met two years ago to talk about his family. A few months earlier his father had walked out, and the divorce battle was just beginning to heat up.

Curtis was thirteen then, in the second half of the eighth grade, an only child living with his mother in the Massachusetts home the family had moved to from New Jersey a couple of years earlier. Still feeling like a new kid in town, his intense intelligence distancing him from his peers, he was so angry about his father's leaving that he adamantly refused to set foot in his new apartment.

"My parents split up and I had to become an adult to fill the gap," he said then. "I'm mad at and dislike both of them equally. I've lost the protection of being a child and I'm

enraged that they'd force their problems onto my life. I feel they use me as a pawn, and I brood a lot. I can't be happy."

Curtis said his parents had been fighting since he was in the sixth grade, and he knew something had to change. But what hurt him the most, he says, is that they sprang the separation on him in the middle of the eighth grade rather than waiting until September—when he'd been planning to go to a new school—as they had promised him.

Although he couldn't see this about himself, Curtis came across as a boy whose intelligence served him fairly well in most situations, but had deserted him when he was most vulnerable. Abandonment and betrayal generate feelings that affect both bright people and not-so-bright ones, but Curtis still felt his brains would help him through the roughest thing he'd had to face in his life. He believed that being away at an academically rigorous boarding school would insulate him against the pain of his parents' breakup. He couldn't understand why they just didn't send him off and then get on with the divorce while he was safely out of the way.

"I just can't concentrate on schoolwork now, and I'm not doing well, and that's affecting my chances to get into prep school," he said.

He was furious that his parents' problems had to mess him up, too. Curtis feels hemmed in now that it's just him and his mother at home. He says he's more aware of her shortcomings and resents the focus she puts on him.

"One of the hardest things is lack of balance, of control, now. My mom, for example, is afraid of dangerous things. She worries about everything and is always trying to tell me what to do. That was okay when my dad was around, because he often had a different viewpoint, but now that it's just her and me, I feel like I'm living under a dictator. There are always fights and standoffs."

Curtis had an interesting perspective on his parents' decision to separate. It was, he says, an admission that they had given up their rights over him.

"When my parents were together they had authority over me, but now they don't," he said.

Because home felt so out of control, Curtis was obsessed with taking charge, and the impulse to do some damage of his own seeps into in his conversation.

"My parents ask me questions about how I'm feeling, details about what I'm doing, but I tell them as little about my life as possible. I want to punish them, and I want to keep part of myself safe. Besides, whenever we start talking it always comes back to the divorce. They couldn't know how this feels, even though they say they want to know. They haven't been in the same situation."

In the middle of the divorce, Curtis couldn't think about anything else, even though he tried to find ways to cope.

"The situation, and how awful it is, is always on my mind. Sometimes I'll do homework, feed the cat, or do laundry, just have some furious burst of action that makes me feel like I'm breaking out of prison."

Curtis had one friend who'd been through divorce, and he felt safe in talking about his situation with him a little bit. But, he admitted, neither of them wanted to get into things too deeply. That sometimes made him wish he had brothers and sisters to discuss things with. But mainly, what he wanted then was for this part of his life to be over.

"I want to find something to do that I like, and then I want to be an independent adult,"
he said.

Two years later, we meet again, and Curtis seems so different. He's taller and slimmer, a vigorous and handsome fifteen-year-old who now commutes to a school where he's finishing the tenth grade. He seems astonished when I tell him the thing I remember most about our earlier meeting is his rage. I'm surprised at how he's replaced it with what seems at first like a positive attitude. But as he talks, something else seeps into his words, a sense of defeat that he assumes is his own fault.

"Yes, I have visited my father's apartment. It was a long time ago, probably just after we

*talked the first time. I sort of decided, 'why
not?' I couldn't really hold a grudge or be
stubborn for too long. It didn't seem to serve
much purpose for me.*

*"I still haven't spent a night there. But I
have met his girlfriend and her family. I don't
have much problem with my father's place anymore,"* he says.

He sounds reasonable when he says this, but underneath the intellectualization there's something else.

*"I don't really feel much anger towards him
anymore, not for divorcing. It just went away.
I realized I should have worked harder at school
that year than I did. I feel it was their choice,
their own lives. I don't feel there's much to be
angry with them about—they were both unhappy in the marriage."*

But Curtis says the anger flares up when his parents
argue or when one of them, particularly his mother,
tries to provoke a fight.

*"I do feel angry, especially with my mother,
when they get me involved in arguments between them. She accuses me of trying to keep
my father's secrets from her, whatever they are.
I don't know how she sees that I'm doing that,
but it's apparently maddening to her,"* he says.

*"Actually, I feel myself drawn more and
more into their disagreements. My mother often
tells me about the arguments she had with him
when they were married and tells me she's just*

trying to protect me from what she knows of him. My dad set up an appointment for me to see a psychologist, and my mother was very suspicious of that. She felt I was going there to complain about her.

"When my father comes to my house, I talk to him away from my mother and she feels excluded. He calls me every night and takes me on vacations and I think my mother feels jealous about that."

Curtis has been riding a bucking horse since his parents separated, a horse he can only control when other things are going well for him. His initial anger softened a bit that first summer when he found success working as a camp counselor. That was followed by a happy first year at his new school, where he made friends and enjoyed the small, supportive classes. But this past year, his second at the school, has been a bust.

"It just changed. I don't feel at home there anymore. I think it's me, because I don't see everyone else changing, and I'm trying to find out why," he says.

Some psychological testing has helped Curtis understand himself a little more.

"I'm pretty disorganized, so I need a lot of structure and I don't have that at home. And the tests show I can be constricted or moody— put up a good front or let everything just fall

apart. I guess I'm not the best child to have in the house."

As a way of coping with everything that's changed, Curtis has learned to look at his parents in quite different ways than he did when the family was intact.

"It's not really better with my mother. We both feel we're the head of the house and neither of us likes it when the other says he or she is. That's a big power struggle. But I have my own room and I do whatever I want, and so does she. We coexist. We watch TV together sometimes, but that's it," he says.

Most adolescent boys need to distance themselves from their mothers and Curtis is obviously trying to do that. He's tougher on her because of that, and because she's the one he lives with.

It's very different with his dad.

"Now that he's not in the house, there's no pressure for him to dominate the family. I can be less family to him and he to me. It's almost like I don't remember what it was like to have a father in the house. I view him as sort of an uncle, and that's kind of good, because it makes me see him more as a real person. Seeing him as a dad, he has to punish me when I do wrong, be responsible for my whole upbringing, and be my role model.

"Not that we have a great relationship. We have fights a lot over petty things and we get

annoyed with each other. Sometimes we have semi-philosophical conversations about things, but I don't tell him what's happened to me during the day."

"I don't think I could have an aunt kind of relationship with my mom if I lived with my dad. I think she'd try to become more maternal. My father has backed off and he acts comfortable with that. She wouldn't back off so easily. I sense she needs me more than he does."

His mother's neediness hobbles Curtis.

"I have something of a responsibility towards her, but I don't feel protective towards her. When it comes down to it, I have to make the decisions that are best for me. If I felt the best thing for me was to go with my father, I would. But changing now would be too upsetting.

"You know, I'm almost sixteen, and I realize you have to look out for your own interests because if you don't, no one else will. Your parents will try to look out for you, but they can't go through life miserable because of you. You have to realize they are their own people."

These are realistic words, even cold, and it makes me feel sad to hear them from Curtis. But then the regret and bitterness come back to his voice.

"With divorce you feel you're alone. You feel your home has been lost and you have to

live with that. I don't think you really know how much you're being changed when it's happening to you. But I think you should probably talk to someone besides your parents about it. It makes what's happening a little clearer."

As he struggles with forming himself in the present, Curtis thinks a bit about the future.

"Sure, I want to get married. But I feel I really need to work on myself before I can fall in love with someone else.

"If I was in a rocky marriage I'd feel like I'd failed. I'd look for some time off. I think that's what my mother had in mind, but that's not what worked out. But I think I'd try to take a month or two off, really try to put things together, to shelter the kids as much as possible. My parents tried, but they didn't really succeed, and I guess I don't know what was best for me, living in a really dysfunctional environment or a divorced family."

Curtis is resigned to the divorce being final.

"I would not be happy if my parents got back together again. It would really change everything. I'd have a father back in the house who I think would try to reclaim his paternal rights. I'd have to deal with much more than my mother's simply being jealous of my father. I wouldn't feel like the house was mine anymore.

"It was the best thing for them to divorce. But I'm not sure it was the best thing for me."

Then Curtis talks about a recent study he says shows that divorce can ruin kids' futures. Still, he thinks he has to take blame for the way he feels.

"I don't say divorce or the lack of a paternal role model have destroyed me. I don't really know what it is. I was doing very well at school—which is basically my life—last year. I wasn't depressed. It just seems to have changed, and now what's happening is that I'm distancing myself from people, telling myself they don't like me. When I think of my career, I don't think I'll end up doing anything I really want to do.

"Last year I was thinking of becoming a writer. This year I flirted with the idea of being a politician. Then I decided I'd rather try to make it in the corporate world and just get money. In the world I've created for myself, that seems to be the road to happiness."

CHAPTER FIVE

DAVE: GRIEF AND STEPPARENTS

Tom May, the head of the guidance department at the high school in Spearfish, South Dakota, reserved a small conference room off the library where I could talk with Dave. My first impression was that this could be a tough interview, that it might take a while for Dave to feel comfortable telling his story.

A stocky sixteen-year-old dressed in a T-shirt and jeans, Dave squirmed in his chair as we introduced ourselves and didn't meet my eyes very easily as I began to explain my project. He looked down and around and held tight to a pile of books in his lap, then stared for a minute at the big clock on the wall and said he'd have to leave when the bell rang. I wondered why Dave had been recommended to me, and if he'd be able to open up and tell me about himself.

I shouldn't have worried. But my instinct that Dave was a boy more at ease with silence than with talking was borne out when he began to divulge the details of his parents' divorce and how he reacted to it. Part of his discomfort may have come from the fact that he's an only child, with no experience of sharing important things with brothers and sisters. But clearly a big part of it was his attempt to bury his pain.

"I didn't talk to anyone at all about the divorce for the first two years. I couldn't bring myself to do it. I wouldn't even talk to my mom. She'd try to talk and I'd just turn away and go somewhere else," Dave said.

Rage had shut him down. That's one way many children of divorce react at first. The anger is so powerful that it blots everything else out and forces you to withdraw into yourself. Doing anything else, reaching out to family or friends, even being receptive to people who stretch out a hand to you, just hurts too much.

Dave might have gone on holding everything close to his heart for years if his guidance counselor, Mr. May, hadn't recognized that he was hurting so badly. He'd noticed Dave's grades had begun to slip and he wondered what was going on. He began to look for him in the halls at school, drawing him out, talking about anything that came to mind at first.

Eventually, Dave felt safe enough to venture into Mr. May's office and break through his wall of silence to talk about what was really bugging him. It was two years after the divorce and it was hard for Dave to take that first step, but it was the beginning of the healing process for him, and one he's grateful to Mr. May for starting.

"The closest person I've been to through the whole ordeal is probably Mr. May. He would get me to talk about things so I'd feel better. He has a way of talking to you on subjects you like, like sports or something, and then leading that into what you need to talk about," Dave explained.

"I'm still pretty angry, but if it hadn't been for Mr. May I wouldn't be talking to you right now. I'd still be bottled up, and I'd be a sophomore, not a junior. My school work was going down the tubes."

Dave knows he was lucky to have an adult who could sense his pain, who wanted to help him find a way to ease it, who knew how to help him get his life going again. It's practically impossible for kids to do that by themselves. Those who don't have the good fortune of having an understanding counselor or teacher or aunt or neighbor in their corner—the majority of kids—can keep on pushing that pain down so deep they don't deal with it for years. But it's there. And it pops up later in life.

A caring adult can help kids deal with not only the pain but the sorrow of divorce. Because divorce is a kind of death—the death of mom and dad's relationship and of the family itself. Grieving over that death is a natural, healthy process. But because society doesn't view divorce with the same sadness it views dying, families and friends don't rally around children left in the wake of sinking marriages. Dave instinctively knew he was on his own when his father left home.

"It would have been easier for me, ten times easier, if one of my parents had died. I love my dad a lot, but it would have been a lot easier on me if he had died in a car wreck than to have him walk right out. Nobody wants to be there for you with divorce," he said.

Dave discovered the hard way something that people who work with children of divorce know very well. Dave would probably have appreciated talking with psychologist Michael Nesson, who counsels many young people in Dave's situation in the Boston area. He knows adults leave kids to grieve on their own.

"One standard thread running through divorce that isn't commonly talked about is children and grief, children and sorrow," Nesson says.

"But there's lots of grief with divorce. Kids see it as abandonment, which it is. And they see themselves at fault, which they aren't.

"It's understandable that a child could view death as an easier thing to deal with than divorce because at least with death you can go through the natural process of grieving. Death is final. Younger children may not understand what's happening when a person has been buried and gone on to some unknown place, but at least there are beliefs in the family that explain the process and make it easier to understand. There's empathy and sorrow and support from other people.

"That doesn't happen with divorce. It's so common that there really isn't much sympathy for kids and what they're going through. The caretaker parent and the child himself and the parent who walked away are all at different levels of healing.

"The problem is that with divorce, the absent person keeps returning, for visits or through court action, and that keeps on opening the wound. Divorce is never over, final, done with. Death is," says Nesson.

Dave was shocked when his father left his mother for another woman when Dave was about thirteen. His dad had gone back to the small town where he'd grown up for a high school reunion, met an old girlfriend, and decided to leave his family for her.

"I had no warning. My mom and dad never fought, never argued. They were happy. But my dad found another woman," Dave explained.

"The thing that made me the maddest was thinking I was the one who caused it. I don't know why; I think every kid thinks that. I thought maybe I'd done something to both of them that just triggered them off. But if I tried to talk with them about that we'd just get into a fight about it.

"I know the reason my dad left because my grandfather told me, but my dad still hasn't told me himself. Even though I know the reason, no matter how you cut it, divorce is painful."

After his father left, Dave and his mother gradually learned to readjust to a new family structure that consisted of just the two of them. His anger kept him from talking with his mother about his feelings, but they got along well enough at home and were there for each other—until his mother met another man, that is, and changed the fragile new family dynamic.

His mom remarried a couple of years after the divorce and his dad, engaged twice since then, is due to be married soon. That's created another complicating factor for Dave: stepparents. Like so many teenagers, he's having a very hard time dealing with new adults assuming old roles in a life he's learned to get used to. He thinks it just isn't their place.

> *"Everything's changed in the house now. I'm still at the point that when my stepdad tries to tell me something I won't do anything for him. Two weeks before he and my mom got married the two of us got into total fisticuffs. He thinks he can tell me what to do, but he can't tell me anything."*

Dave's playing a power game: he doesn't think his stepfather has any right to act like his real father.

> *"He'll never get me to obey if I don't want to. When I'm going out he'll tell me what time to be in and I come in two hours later on purpose. He stays up waiting for me and starts screaming and hollering. But I keep on doing it."*

Dave refuses to accept that his stepfather has any authority in the family, but he also blames his mother for altering the new arrangement they'd learned to live with. He sees her as another enemy now, her remarriage as another betrayal.

"She's supposed to be there for me, not for him," he said.

Psychologist Michael Nesson says Dave's reaction to his parents' dating is as typical as his anger about the divorce.

"There's a lot of trauma involved in seeing your parents dating," Nesson says.

"Kids struggle for the same kind of attention from the parent as the attention the parent is giving to the person he or she is dating. It's very common for kids to act out through aggression, drug use, or other unacceptable behavior when the parent becomes involved with other people."

Dave suspects his mother is becoming aware of how hard it is for him to take orders from a man he sees as having waltzed in and taken his place in the family.

"Lately she's started to tell him that he doesn't have to talk to me, that I'll listen to her. She's learned. Before they were married she sided with him one day and I moved out to my grandpa's for half the summer. They finally got me to come to their wedding, and after that I began to move back in slowly. I won't take

orders from him, but I still try to get along with him just to please Mom."

He tries now to get along with his real father to please himself.

"For two solid years I never saw him. He tried, but I didn't want anything to do with him. Then one day he came to the house and asked me if I'd take a walk with him. I went, and we talked things over, tried to work things out. The past year has been real good," Dave said.

"At first, though, he tried to buy me back. He thought that was the only way he could get me to be with him. Of course it worked for a while. But now he's doing more than buying me stuff. He takes me places and treats me like a friend instead of a son. He's getting married soon, and I'll go to the wedding. Things are okay with him now, but maybe it would have been different if I lived with him and not my mother."

Because talking was so hard for Dave at first, he's reluctant to advise other kids facing divorce to seek a sympathetic ear, even though he knows how helpful Mr. May has been to him. It's just that he knows opening up is so hard.

"I'd tell kids to do what they think they need to do. If they feel like they can talk, then talk. But if they feel like they can't, then wait until they can open up. After a while my mom told me, 'Well, if you don't want to talk about this,

we won't mention it.' That was a lot easier for me. If I was busy and didn't have to think about it, then that was all the better, so I went hunting and fishing with my neighbor and my grandpa. When the time came to think about it, then it was there, and I started to think.''

CHAPTER SIX

RACHAEL: CAUGHT IN THE MIDDLE

When you talk to psychologists or lawyers or guidance counselors, or to any of the other people who come in contact with divorce through their work, you hear a lot about the kids caught in the middle. It's what happens when parents are consumed by their own loss and anger, financial worries, and power games, often to such an extent that they haven't any emotion—or good sense— left to tend to their children.

Rachael is a seventeen-year-old high school junior who lives in Cincinnati. She's a beautiful young woman with long glossy black hair who marches on the drill team at school, has friends, and gets lots of attention from boys because of her looks. But her family is in shambles.

"The advice I'd give to kids whose parents are splitting up is this: don't get in the middle of their divorce," says Rachael, speaking softly

in a tiny meeting room near the principal's office of her school.

"I've found myself in that spot a lot. My mom and dad don't talk to each other. My mom will tell me to tell my dad something and then he'll tell me to do something. It makes me mad. Sometimes I don't think they realize they're doing it. They're too busy trying to make each other mad," Rachael said.

Rachael's dad now lives with his mother across the street from Rachael, her mother, and her brother Ricky.

"Actually he's been over there for a long time. Before, he'd go over there for maybe a month and we wouldn't even know he was gone, so his leaving isn't anything new.

"But now he asks me to come and live with him and I don't know if it's because he loves me or is still trying to get back at my mom for the divorce. That makes me feel confused and frustrated," Rachael said.

"Sometimes I think about it because I want to be closer to my dad. I think it might help me a lot. I've never had a relationship with him. My mom used to tell me that he wouldn't ever hold me when I was a baby. She said he started having problems when I was born. My mom says that the way he was raised, the first child was always favored. I was the third girl. So my oldest sister was favored, and the second oldest and I were in the middle. I don't blame myself.

"My mom thinks it would hurt me if I went to live with my dad. When I'm with him, all he does is talk about my mom. He goes on and on. Sometimes I think he just wants to make her mad. He's not supposed to be on our property, but sometimes I think he comes into the house. It would probably be a lot easier for my mom if he lived in a different town."

Rachael was fifteen when her parents' long-standing problems came to a head. She knew they argued, she said, but she always tried to block out the fighting.

"I came home from school one day and there were two police officers there and a police car outside the house. I don't remember what they were talking about. They handcuffed my dad and just left and stuck him right in jail. He blamed it all on my mom, but he lies to me. I don't know if he thinks I'll forget or if he just sees it in a different way or he's just trying to make me believe him.

"Not that I can remember my parents ever getting along. My dad has a lot of mental problems. My mom tries to tell me about them. He has obsessive-compulsive disorder. He doesn't think he does, but he used to wash his hands so much they'd bleed. He thought they were dirty. He used to take medicine for it. At the custody trial, he had a psychiatrist testify there wasn't anything wrong with him. But I know there is."

Rachael says she sensed from the time she was a little girl that her parents would leave each other eventually.

"I know my dad still loves my mom a lot and she loves him, but they have so many problems they just can't communicate. They blame each other and no one wants to take responsibility.

"Actually they aren't officially divorced yet. First it was the custody trial. I have two older sisters in their twenties who don't live at home anymore and a seven-year-old brother, Ricky. I didn't have to testify in the courtroom, but my brother and I talked to the judge. The judge asked me how I thought about my mom and dad, where I wanted to live, who I got along with better, who I could talk to. I said my mom. I was never very close to my dad."

But even though she and Ricky live with her mom and will after the divorce is final, Rachael's relationship with her mother has changed in many ways, as has her position in the family. The separation has brought financial pressure on both parents, and Rachael and her sisters and brother are suffering the consequences.

"Sometimes I can talk to my mom, but lately, in the last year, we've had a lot of problems. She's a nurse and she has to work a lot at night, sometimes twelve-hour shifts. She works so much that when she has free time she spends most of it with my brother. We don't get

*the chance to hang out together very much. I'm
on the drill team and she used to come to games,
but she doesn't have time for that anymore. My
dad doesn't come either.*

*"Now that my sisters have moved out,
sometimes I have to stay home with my brother.
I don't really like staying home. Ricky is ten
years younger than me and sometimes I feel like
I have to be a mom to him. We worry he's going
to act like a girl because he's been brought up
with all of us. He's never been close to my dad.*

*"I worry about Ricky. He has nervous prob-
lems, twitches his eyes and snaps his fingers
when he gets mad. I try to be a good big sister
and he has other people to take care of him,
but I don't think it will ever make up for* [the
loss of] *my dad."*

Rachael doesn't really think there's anyone taking
care of her, either. "This divorce won't be over for a
long time. They just argue back and forth about the
house and who's going to get what and it takes so long
to get a court date. When they get one, sometimes my
dad won't show up. When he does come they can't
come to an agreement. My dad pays his legal bills and
my mom's still paying for hers. She's trying to get
herself out of debt, but I think she's going to be paying
for a long time."

Rachael's mother may not be able to talk with her
daughter in the way Rachael would like, but she knows
Rachael needs help in dealing with the family's problems and she's urged her to get it.

"We've all reacted differently in the family. One of my sisters is away at college and just doesn't want to talk about it. The other one is hurt by it. I don't really talk about it much, although my mother wants me to. I've been to a counselor a lot, with my mom's support, to deal with it.

"At first I didn't mind going to the psychologist and I thought it was helpful. But now I don't really want to. I'm in a divorce group at school and that's better because there are kids there who've been through the same thing. Not exactly, you know, but divorce. I prefer the group. I find it easier to talk there.

"For a while I was seeing a psychiatrist to help me deal with my anger. I would throw tantrums and not let the anger out. I'd just keep it all inside, and when something happened, say with a teacher, I'd just blow up and get in trouble and even get suspended. I don't do that much anymore. I've changed, learned to control my anger a little better."

Despite the pain, Rachael doesn't wish her parents had divorced long ago, and wishes even now that it didn't have to happen to her family.

"I just wish things had been different, that my dad didn't have problems, that my mom didn't have problems of her own. But I don't fantasize about them getting back together.

"What I do fantasize about is the perfect

family,'' Rachael said, tears streaming down her face.

I ask her what the perfect family looks like.

"It's a father having a job. A mother having a job. Both of them with stable jobs, saving their money, liking what they do. Being happy with the kids they raised and everyone getting along. None of my friends have that."

When she looks ahead, Rachael wants to see marriage for herself, but suspects it will take her a while to find the right partner.

"I have problems with boys now," she said. *"But I do think it's possible to have a good marriage if you have good morals and raise your kids right. Maybe when I get married I'll do some things differently. First, I'll find the right husband, somebody who's nice and respects me and is handsome. My parents don't respect each other.*

"I really think my parents got married because they loved each other and they do love each other, but a lot of things changed. I don't really know what went wrong."

Usually kids don't know what went wrong. Often, during the divorce and maybe for years afterward, they are manipulated into becoming messengers of ill will from one parent to another. They're treated like pieces of property in custody battles. They're forced to become mediators between a mom and dad at war with each other, to make choices no child should have to make. The battlefield is a terrible place to be.

The experts say that one of the unwritten laws of divorce is: The more contentious and ugly the breakup, the harder it is for children to cope. By the same token, the more contact children have with both parents all along the way, the more likely that they will eventually come to grips with the inevitable losses and be able to accept new families in rearranged forms.

Florence Goldfield has seen that. A Massachusetts psychologist and lawyer, she is often called in by judges in divorce cases to help resolve child-custody and visitation issues. Her job is to help decide what is in the child's best interest.

"The more amicable and friendly a divorce is, the less hostility there is, the better it is for the kids," Goldfield says. "There's no question about that. But still, that doesn't diminish the fundamental impact of losing two parents. Divorce makes you realize you can lose. Kids become frightened for themselves. If you can lose a parent, you can lose anyone. Nothing in life is certain.

"Unfortunately, what I see a lot of the time is that kids are just the subject matter of a case, like property. The parents have rights, but kids don't. Legally, kids could and should have rights, but who would exercise them? The parents always prevail."

CHAPTER SEVEN

SUZANNE AND BRIAN: MAKING THE MOST OF IT

As far as most children are concerned, there's neither a good time nor a good age to be for divorce to happen. But it does. Thirty years ago about 10 in 1,000 marriages failed. In the 1990s, the rate is about 21 per 1,000. That statistic translates into over one million children a year who have to endure the breakup of their families. Many of them get very little help.

But like most things in life, divorce can have a positive side, too. Some kids learn they can handle things they didn't think they could. They have to deal with issues and feelings they wouldn't have had to otherwise. They see they can survive and they grow from that.

That's Suzanne's situation. She's fourteen, a ninth-grader in Connecticut. Although her situation isn't perfect, she considers herself a lucky survivor of divorce. Her parents split up when she was just three, but now both are married again and all four parents get along with each other.

"I think if parents are going to divorce, they should do it while the kids are little. I was so young when they told me, three years old, that I ran out of the house because I wanted to tell my best friend the news. I didn't know what was happening or that it was a bad thing. I think it must be more of a shock when you're older," Suzanne says.

Because she was too young to have lived with her parents in an intact family for very long before the divorce, Suzanne doesn't feel the same degree of loss or pain as do kids who are older when the breakup comes. She doesn't remember the good times, or the bad. Maybe her feelings have just been scarred over.

"My mom says she and my dad just lost interest in each other. They had dated since junior high, but they came to a point where they didn't love each other anymore. She tried to hold it together but it just didn't work. They didn't fight.

"I stayed with my mother and my dad moved to a house three streets away. I used to go over there all the time during the week when I was younger. Now that I'm older and my life is busier, I just go on the weekends. I see him less than I did before," Suzanne said.

The family has changed too.

"Both my parents have married again and besides my sister, who's two years older than

me, I have an eleven-year-old stepbrother, my mom's husband's son. I feel kind of sorry for him, because he lives in a lot of places. His mom is divorced a second time and he doesn't talk much about it. He confides in me the most, which isn't much. When I ask if he wants to talk he usually says no. After a while he talks more, but it's hard to get much out of him. I say, 'Sam, I know how it is'. So even though we're not that close now, I feel as though I've gained a brother.''

In contrast to many other adolescents, Suzanne's stepparent grievances are pretty minor, and although she complains a little, she thinks she's pretty lucky with how things have turned out. She realizes that although her parents divorced, both continued to take responsibility for their children, and both showed that their love wouldn't stop just because the family had been rearranged. Still, there are annoyances. Suzanne says her stepmother's rules are different from her real mother's and she still has to adjust when she moves from home to home.

"I admit I react sometimes to my stepmother's strict rules by saying, 'Well, my mom doesn't do that.' I think steps have a right to yell but not to punish, but that's only happened three times. Now my stepmom leaves disciplining up to my dad. She's usually fun, like an older sister, but she needs everything to be neat. She just doesn't have any experience with kids.''

Despite the strain of adapting to different parenting styles, Suzanne says there have been benefits of divorce for her.

"I like my parents and my stepparents. When I think of family I think of all of them, the whole thing. Everyone's the same. That's a benefit, so I'd have to say that for me, some good things came from the divorce. I got a lot of extra cousins—and extra presents at Christmas."

Suzanne's parents make an effort to provide unified support for their children, and that has made a big difference in the way they've been able to cope. One of her school's counselors, Barry Lewis, who also has a private family counseling practice, says he doesn't see many parents like Suzanne's. He wishes he did.

"I've seen people motivated to make changes, really working hard not to do the same things that got them in trouble. They've educated themselves through reading or they've gone into therapy. The kids who come out of divorce well tend to be the ones with parents like that," Lewis says.

Suzanne says her parents have always been emotionally available to her.

"We've always been able to talk about things, and I think it's better that way. It's not good to keep everything inside," she said.

The two families get along so well, in fact, that they make a combined vacation an annual event.

"We have a big family outing with everyone every year. My mom and dad and their new spouses and all the kids go to my dad's place in Vermont. My mom and dad are almost like best friends, they're that close. It's always been that way. The steps get along well too."

Some kids haven't had the support and the expanded family that Suzanne has had; nevertheless there's been enough parental help and enough time has passed since the divorce to allow them to handle life in a responsible way. Are some of them just postponing the pain?

"There are kids who come out of divorce very well. Some focus on school or sports and achievements and ignore what's happening at home. But it may become harder to cope when they get older if they haven't dealt with the issues at the time. We certainly know now that divorce has lasting effects," says counselor Barry Lewis.

"While the divorce rate was soaring in the 1970s and 1980s, adults justified it on the grounds that it was better for them, that change and a new start were good things. People didn't fool themselves that it would be easy for anyone, but they believed the children would recover after a year or two and get their lives back on track without suffering permanent scars. Now, many are beginning to see it differently.

"Divorce might be better for the parents, but I

don't know if the kids ever see it as being better,'' says Barry Lewis.

''Kids grow up thinking the world is supposed to be one way and divorce shatters that belief system. It takes a lot of time for them to incorporate those changes and to create a new belief system. Maybe later they can see it was necessary, but at the time it's happening, they don't.''

The disruption and inescapable changes of divorce affect children in different ways, depending on how old they are at the time, how the parents handle the breakup, and how much security the parents are able to provide in the years that follow.

Some kids, like Suzanne, get lucky. They're certainly not in the majority and they'd be the first to tell you that no matter how smoothly it goes, divorce is never a happy event. Kids may not realize it, but it's just as painful for their parents, at least in the short run. Anger, guilt, and rejection can eat up adults too, which is why so many of them have little emotional energy left for their children.

But luck can come with divorce in a couple of ways. You might be one of the unusual ones whose parents want to separate but who manage to be civil about the process and take your feelings into consideration. Adults who can explain what's going on, who don't get bogged down in bitter fighting, and who have some respect for each other can support their children and those children can survive divorce better. But too many parents aren't mature enough for this.

Other kids are lucky in a different way. Many

schools, churches, and youth groups are so aware of the high divorce rate that they run support groups. At these safe havens kids can talk with others in the same situation about their feelings and their problems. This can be tremendously helpful. You can learn a lot from someone who's been through what you're experiencing, and that can make it easier for you to cope.

"I've seen horrendous situations in which kids suffer depression and anxiety for a long time. They show depression in different ways. Some are overtly lethargic and withdrawn. They don't talk and they aren't happy. Others can act out more as a way of defending themselves or covering up. Sometimes I can see the sadness underneath and know a child is in a lot of pain," says Barry Lewis.

Brian's situation isn't as comforting as Suzanne's, but he's come to terms with the path his family life has taken so far. He appears to be a boy who's focusing on his own future and refusing to acknowledge his pain. He's fourteen, lives in Florida with his mother and older brother, and even though it's been several years since he's seen his father, he's been able to create a life of his own.

Brian's mother has been a constant in his life. She's a hard worker who spends time with her sons and is emotionally sympathetic. She's dated a little since her divorce but hasn't been serious about another man, so Brian hasn't had to contend with a stepfather. The family has settled into a safe and happy routine. Since he hasn't had to face sharing his mother, perhaps it's easier for Brian to say he wouldn't mind if she had more of a social life.

"I'm very close to my mom—I can talk to her about most things. She isn't dating anyone, but I don't see anything wrong with it if she does. It's better for her to do things, have a social life, better than not doing anything," he said.

Brian is small for his age and I'm not surprised when he says he's a wrestler in the lightweight division at his high school. He speaks openly and deliberately about his father, as though the man is not quite real. He leans forward in his seat and smiles when he reveals the dreams and plans he's forging for himself. Somehow, he's been able to channel his loss into positive paths. Maybe he's just got the luck of the Irish.

"Both my parents are from Ireland. My dad lives there now. I never see him. He sends birthday cards and around Christmas he sends cards, too. But that's not really so different from when he was living with us. He was away from us enough, working at jobs in other cities, that I sort of got used to not having him around. I think it would be more painful for me if he'd written a lot and then stopped, but I guess he never really did write that much.

"I was in the fourth grade when my parents divorced. I didn't want it to happen, but as I said, he was working in other places anyway so I didn't get to see him that much. We used to visit him for two months in the summer before he moved back to Ireland. The year I was eleven we went to Ireland and one of my aunts brought

*us to meet him and we visited for a while, but
I haven't seen him since.*

> *"I miss not being able to see my dad all the
> time, do things with him. My friends do things
> with their dads. But I've gotten so used to not
> having him around. Besides, my brother is good
> and supportive."*

Brian's mother has made it a point not to discredit
her ex-husband to the children, which has probably
contributed to Brian's positive attitude.

> *"My mom's careful not to run my dad
> down. If she started insulting him I'd probably
> be against him, too. I'm kind of neutral. But I
> would like to ask him what he's been doing all
> these years, and tell him what I've been doing.
> I have some sad memories of before the divorce.
> Mom didn't like his drinking and they'd fight.
> He'd stop sometimes. I wouldn't ask him why he
> hasn't been around because I know Mom didn't
> want him near us while he was drinking."*

Brian's family life changed in several ways after
the divorce. Most children keep on living with their
mothers, who either have to begin working or spend
longer hours on the job than they did before. Some
fathers who agree in court to provide child support are
late with their checks, or stop sending much money at
all. Supporting two households is always more expen-
sive than one.

> *"When I was younger my mother didn't
> work. But after she became a single parent she*

always had to. At first she worked just a half
day, but then she had to go full time. So we had
baby-sitters after school. You got to know the
sitter and you liked them and liked coming home
to the same person and then they'd leave and
you'd start with a new one. I didn't like that.

   "Money is somewhat of an issue," Brian
said.

   "Other people get a lot of stuff for Christ-
mas. I get a good amount, but nothing special.
It bothers me somewhat. My dad doesn't send
money for us."

Brian's grown out of some of the earlier stages,
such as adjusting to new baby-sitters. Now, as a member of the high school wrestling team, he stays late
after school when his sport is in season. As a member
of the Key Club, he gets involved in service projects
such as cleaning up the beach, and he goes with the
club on ice skating parties and ski trips to Colorado.
He's got friends, and he's busy, and all of that helps.

   He's also ambitious, and that channels his energy.
He studies hard and definitely wants to go to college
so he can get a good job.

   "My plan now is engineering. I'm taking
all the right courses, keeping my grade point
average up. Maybe I'll go to graduate school
after that. I want to get started on a career and
I definitely don't want to be in my mother's
economic situation.

   "I feel more mature and focused than other

kids my age. Some of my friends act sort of stupid, but I hang around with a nice crowd.

Still, sometimes he feels a little removed.

"I don't want to talk with them about the divorce, though. They don't really know about it. They don't even think much about divorce because they haven't gone through it. I've heard some of them say their parents have come close to separating, and I know kids who have divorced parents, but they aren't my close friends."

Brian doesn't harbor any illusions that his parents will get back together.

"I don't even think my mom will marry again, although I don't have anything against that. I do know she'd never marry someone who would be mean to her or us again. She doesn't talk about being lonely."

Knowing how marriage can end hasn't made Brian shy away from thinking about it for himself someday.

"I would like to get married and have kids and a good family. I don't really worry about making a commitment to the family. I think I'll be able to. I'm different from my dad. I don't want to drink, although I know most teenagers do.

"I think the key to a good marriage is to be close to your wife and don't drink. The main

thing is that I want to have enough money to support my family so that one of us can be around for the kids. I don't want my wife to have to work unless she chooses to, if she's been to college and wants to work. I'd rather have one of us stay home with the kids while they're growing up because I think kids need that.''

Brian has done something that psychologists say is healthy when you're dealing with the loss that comes from divorce. He's aligned himself with his mother and takes strength from her support. He's involved himself in school and community activities. He's been able to make goals for himself, to think of ways he can shape his own life.

''I just have one bit of advice for kids going through it,'' said Brian, thinking carefully about what he could say that might mean something to another kid.

''Stay close to the parent you live with. If you're going to live with her, then you might as well agree with her and not fight. That will just mess you up more. You've got to think about the future.''

CHAPTER EIGHT

JOANIE:
THE WRANGLING NEVER ENDS

Joanie was seventeen when we talked, four years away from her parents' breakup, and to her, it all still seemed like a nightmare.

> *"They first separated when I was thirteen, but technically the divorce wasn't final until last year. And the fighting still goes on,"* she said.

Joanie lives in Albany, New York, but I met her at the boarding school in Connecticut where she's a senior. Lack of money hasn't been the problem in her family as it is in so many other broken homes. She lives on a lovely campus where narrow tree-lined paths link redbrick dormitories and classroom buildings. She's getting the very best prep school education and planning on going to college. In this idyllic setting, she's usually able to ignore the day-to-day turmoil at home, but not always.

> *"My mom uses me as a pawn in the money battles. My father tries to manipulate me, and*

I wish I could be more forceful with him. How can I deal with all this and senior year, too? Sometimes I can laugh at the ridiculousness of it—the lies, anger, all of it—and I can block it out. I try to step aside and realize it's just the two of them fighting and that it really doesn't have a lot to do with me. But it's only okay for a little while at a time."

Frances Goldfield, the Massachusetts psychologist and lawyer who's had years of experience with families on the skids, knows lots of families like Joanie's. She agrees that the messier the divorce, the longer it takes for everyone involved to recover. Her work puts her in a position to see feuding parents and anguished kids who end up back in court years after the divorce, long after things were supposedly settled. Why does the confusion and pain go on for so long?

"The big reason divorce is so difficult is that very often the problems between the parents aren't really resolved at the time of the breakup. And an unresolved divorce is never final," Goldfield says. The judge may have settled questions like who gets the house and who pays for braces, which parent the kids will live with, and how much dad pays in child support and college tuition, but down deep, the real issues haven't been put on the table. What was going on in the family? Festering bitterness, Goldfield says, often draws people back to the courtroom.

"Some people just have to get back up on the witness stand and testify about all the bad things that have been done to them. It's got to come out. It's like lancing a boil, and if it isn't done, it keeps on coming out like a million little boils." And it keeps on prolonging the disruption for kids.

Joanie's parents' divorce didn't come as a big shock to her or her younger sister.

> *"They were always fighting, so I knew they'd divorce someday. One day, after a particularly bad week, my mom told me and my sister, who's five years younger than me, to pack our bags because we were leaving. We stayed with friends for a few days while my dad made plans to move out, but it ended up taking him nearly a month until he found his own apartment.*

> *"They both said the separation was going to be on a trial basis, but that was the biggest lie I ever heard. They may have believed it. They tried therapy and talking, but six months later they were still fighting—over the phone and by letter. It got so bad that now they don't even talk to each other at all. They haven't for three years."*

Joanie's parents battled over the standard issues— custody and money.

> *"It was the same thing over and over again. Mom was awarded custody of my sister and me. Then two and a half years after that, my dad was back in court looking for joint custody. I*

was away at school by that time and I didn't want to go back home to go to court. Besides, I just knew I'd feel guilty for both sides.

"The joint custody didn't happen and I know my dad still appeals money decisions in court."

Joanie watched her parents act like children and she's struggled not to let their behavior retard her own developing maturity. After the years of wrangling, she has no illusions that her parents are truly capable, or willing, to set aside their feelings for each other and look out for her.

"I learned that parents lie. I first thought my dad was lying to me about my mom and that would make me angry, but then I'd find her doing the same thing. They make a lot of false promises, too. It's a way of trying to keep you on their side. My dad told me he'd buy a new house so I could have a new room. He tried to paint a picture of what he thought I wanted. I've found it's best to stay out of it, not to let them make me feel guilty."

Joanie's father has married again. His new wife, twenty years younger than he is, was a single mother with two children in their early teens and, at the time I met Joanie, a new baby was on the way. Joanie might be able to like her if her mom didn't work so hard to bad-mouth her and accuse her of causing money troubles for the whole clan.

"I don't really have a reason to hate my stepmother, but I'm influenced by my mom. As for my dad, I don't think he's reacted too well to the new relationships. He has this image of a perfect family and thought he could have that when he remarried. He wants us to like his new wife, but he doesn't understand that it just doesn't suddenly flow, that you don't bond right away. He blames me and my sister if things don't go as well as he expects. None of them understand how hard it is for us.

"Here's a good example. My dad knows I love to read, so he found a place for me to read in his new house and thought that would make me happy. He tries hard to make me feel comfortable there, but since I only go there three or four times a year I don't have a room of my own. A reading corner isn't going to do it."

Although she's glad she's away at school, Joanie worries about her sister, who goes back and forth between her mother's town house and her father's new home and family.

"I'm removed from the day-to-day of it, kind of like an observer, but she has to deal with it. She could be having fun at her age now, but I don't think she is. I'm afraid that we've grown apart since I've been here. It seems like our only bond now is to talk about our dad, and we've had different opinions about him.

"My sister used to think the new family was

great, and I'd get annoyed. But now sometimes she complains about them. She says she's always getting blamed by our stepmom for things that go wrong. She feels left out. She's only at their house on weekends and she just hears about the great things they're doing, like going skiing out west. They never tell her they're doing those things but she finds out from our stepbrother and stepsister. My dad lies; he says he's going to a convention or something, but he's really taking them all skiing."

Joanie says that for her, even though she doesn't spend much time at either house, bouncing between them only underscores the differences in the way her parents live now.

"My mom works long days now and she lives in a town house. My dad built a fancy modern house and he and his wife party, go out to dinner, and have a fun lifestyle that makes them seem as though they believe nothing much matters. Enjoy what you have, be carefree — that's their attitude. My dad doesn't have the daily concerns like who's going to take us to the doctor. Then my mom wants the details of what happened while I was at my dad's house. Something always happens, but I don't want to tell her everything."

Joanie's father is full of promises—about visiting her at school, traveling together, incorporating her into his new family. But, she says, he doesn't know how to follow through and only hurts her each time he lets her down. She worries that she's too much like him.

"We have a lot of the same personality characteristics," she said.

"He keeps his real feelings to himself and I trap mine inside, so we don't tell each other much. We both find it hard to talk about personal things, the little connections. We've grown apart in the last few years because of that.

"I used to talk with him every day about baseball; it was something he taught me about and the only real bond we had. I'm afraid to stop talking about that now because if I do, what will be left?"

Because she feels like she's losing her father, Joanie expresses her feelings for him by asking him for his time, even though she's gotten used to his failed promises.

"He says he'll come up to school to see me but he doesn't. He's passive, and his new wife controls what they do. She has no interest in seeing me. Even though I've told him I want him to come, he doesn't. He promised to come to college night so I told my mom not to come, and then he ducked out at the last minute. He said something else came up. I think he wants to make me happy but he just doesn't know how to do that."

At one point a few years ago, the quarreling with her father about their relationship burned her out.

"I just couldn't speak to him for six weeks. I resolved that I wouldn't talk anymore so I wouldn't have to deal with being hurt. The peaks and valleys are so hard. He wrote me at camp that summer begging me to call him—he can't understand why the disappointments hurt so much," Joanie said.

Divorce has made Joanie wary of marriage for herself, a sentiment she expressed to her mother one day while they were driving in the car.

"I told her last year that I'd never marry or have kids and she pulled the car over and looked at me and asked if it was the result of the divorce. She said she couldn't really understand my feelings because it had been a good thing for her. It made her stronger.

"But I told her that all I could see was their anger and I wouldn't want to be that angry with a person I loved, or hurt my kids as much as they're hurting my sister and me."

Joanie sees changes in herself that she traces back to the divorce, and she doesn't like them. But she's getting better about expressing her feelings in the divorce support group she attends at school every week.

"I don't trust people as much as I should now. I'm more self-conscious than I used to be, and I wonder about the motives of people who

want to be friends. I was always afraid to express anger in a friendship because I was afraid that might end it, but now I'm more willing to take that risk. I don't know if that's good or bad.

"At first I was going for therapy, but I couldn't express myself. I didn't really trust the professionals, I guess. I thought they'd tell my mother everything I told them. So I've learned to cope in different ways.

"I have a few friends I've mentioned things to. But most has come out in my writing, and then through the support group. I was really timid about going there at first, when I was a tenth-grader, but I've found it to be really helpful and now I look forward to it. It's the best thing that has happened to me. There are a range of people in the group and an adult, who's been divorced, leads the discussions.

"We just talk, and it helps me to feel less alone. I feel like I've been through so much: custody, money, stepparents. I want to be able to get to a place where I can feel as though I'm over it and can begin to help others who are going through it.

"I'd tell other kids that I learned parents lie. It's best to stay out of their arguments and not to fall for the guilt trips they try to trap you in."

The continued fighting means Joanie can't get on with her own life, she feels, and it makes it hard for

her to plan for the important moments of her life that
are coming up.

"I can't see them ever resolving their prob-
lems. So what do I do at graduation, or if I
ever get married? How can they sit in the same
room? What am I going to do? Graduation's
coming up and I wonder where they'll sit. Will
I worry all day about allotting enough time to
both of them? It never ends."

Joanie's parents have too many issues still flaming
between them. Her father sounds like he's trying to
hang on to his youth and his youthful visions of the
perfect life. Her mother is filled with bitterness. And
so the turmoil continues.

"He says that once the divorce is final, life
can only get better. She says once the money is
settled, life can only get better. I don't see them
ever coming to grips with the real issues."

CHAPTER NINE

ERIC: DENIAL

Eric is like a young deer frozen in the headlights of a speeding truck on a rainy highway. His eyes are dull behind thick glasses. He sags into a plastic-backed chair in his guidance counselor's office so he can tell me his story. His counselor has informed me that his mother left the family a year earlier, when Eric was twelve. I've been warned that he's listless and is handling the divorce by denying that it's causing him pain.

When he arrives he doesn't appear particularly interested in talking, but he's not disinterested either—he's just there, his tuna sandwich and potato chips from the cafeteria on a plastic tray in front of him. A bad cold can be heard in his voice, and he responds to my questions in a flat tone, with short answers devoid of much detail.

I recall that depression, according to psychologists, is a common way to cope with divorce. You zone out, tell yourself that what's happening isn't such a huge deal, that you can keep on going without being affected by the real world. For a while, that gives you the illusion you're handling things well. But denying reality now is likely to betray you later in life, usually when you try to get close to someone else.

I suspect Eric is zoning out. He gives the details of his situation but keeps his feelings very well hidden.

"I didn't talk about it in the beginning because I didn't have any reason to talk," he says.

"I just kept to myself, and that worked for me. I like to keep my life to myself. I think some kids want to be depressed about divorce. People just like to feel sorry for themselves."

Eric says his parents delivered the news of their breakup calmly. It sounds as though even then he was denying what was happening.

"They called me into the kitchen. They told me they couldn't live with each other anymore, that they weren't going to fight or anything. They were just going to get divorced.

"At first I thought they'd just separate and that would last for a month or two and then they'd get back together. But it's been almost a year now. And my mom has remarried.

"She was the moving party. I don't think my dad would have left if she hadn't. But he really doesn't talk to me about those things. I don't know how he feels about it. I just think that my mom isn't the only awful one. My dad has his faults, too.

Eric is an only child who didn't notice any tensions building between his parents before his mother decided to leave after twenty-three years of marriage. Was he blotting out the things he didn't want to see? Or maybe his parents simply drifted apart in a quiet way, so quietly there wasn't much for Eric to notice.

"I didn't know what was going on in their marriage. They didn't argue, but there wasn't any great romance, either. It's been like that all my life. I think I would have preferred it if they had argued and then gotten divorced."

Even though it was a shock, Eric says he took the breakup pretty casually at first.

"For the first three or four months I had no problem with it. But then I started to miss seeing my mom. I missed my parents being together and stuff like that, and my grades started to slip. It was tough for me to get back on track. I have to be a lot more responsible at home now. That's tough."

Divorce has changed Eric's daily routine. Now that he and his dad are living like a couple of bachelor roommates, he has had to assume many of the household duties his mother used to handle. He's not crazy about that.

"I miss my mom's help. I miss the things she did for me, like make the bed. I have to do that now and it's a pain in the butt. I have to help with dinner, clean the house. My dad gets

home at five-thirty or six so he doesn't have much time to do that kind of stuff during the week. My mom used to get home the same time I did from school.''

Eric says he misses his mother's presence and her help but never admits what he really misses is his mother, period. In fact, he makes a pretty big point of saying he doesn't miss her all that much.

"I'm not really lonely now that she's not there. It gives me more time to do my home-work. I wish she was still around to help me with history and English, though.''

Eric's parents don't argue in front of him now that they've split up, but neither do they try hard for his sake to keep up the front of a good relationship.

"How do my parents get along now? 'Hello, how are you, good-bye.' They try not to use me as a pawn. They try not to argue, or to do it away from me. But when they get started on the phone with each other I just hang it up and walk away.''

I try to envision what dinner is like at Eric's house and see a boy and his father sitting together trying to make conversation but neither of them asking the questions they want to ask or expressing the feelings that need to be expressed. Between them sits the ghost of a missing person.

"I get along with my dad okay. I can talk to him—when I have something to talk about.

*We talk during dinner about boating and stuff.
He's a great sailor. I'm sure he could ask me
about how I feel but I wouldn't want him to.''*

Eric's mother has married a man she worked with,
someone she had known for three years before she left
the family. Eric says he thinks her remarriage was a
good thing—for her. But he fears it takes her another
step farther away from him, which he doesn't like.

> *"I don't like having to share my time with
> her and her new husband. He's nice enough,
> but he's not a real sensitive guy. He has a three-
> year-old son who lives with his mom.
> "Charlie, the little boy, likes it when we go
> over to my mom's house at the same time be-
> cause we have more fun. Sometimes I like being
> a big brother, but having this kid is not really
> a benefit of the divorce. I'd rather have some-
> one my own age I could talk to. I think all of
> this would probably have been easier if I had a
> brother or a sister.
> "Every once in a while I get angry at my
> stepdad. He does things I don't like, so we get
> in loud arguments. But they don't last long. In
> some ways I guess I resent him for taking my
> father's place."*

Eric's lunch hour is over but he's barely touched
the sandwich on his plate. He has talked, but has re-
vealed more about himself by what he's left out. He
seems awfully sad. But when I ask him what advice
he'd give other kids facing divorce his answer carries

the same hard-nosed edge that a lot of his comments do.

> *"My advice to someone going through divorce is just to live with it. I don't think there's any need to talk about it. People just feel sorry for themselves. I don't get depressed."*

CHAPTER TEN

EDUARDO: TOO MUCH ABUSE

"The whole family and my father's friends knew it would happen eventually because of what my father was up to. He was fooling around and lying to my mom, and everybody knew it."

Eduardo was seventeen when we met. He's a tall kid with black hair and a reserved attitude. His tales of the violence and alcohol he's witnessed seem shocking because he's so calm as he tells them.

He's the middle child of a family of five that had broken up six years earlier, when Eduardo was eleven. He's lived his whole life in a Boston neighborhood that sits in the shadows of historic colonial landmarks. It is a close-knit community where people know you, and your extended family often lives just around the corner. Although it's a nurturing atmosphere, the closeness wasn't enough to keep Eduardo's parents together. He puts the blame squarely on his father's broad shoulders.

"They were always fighting," says Eduardo.

"One night there was one big fight and my mom called the cops, although that wasn't the first time she'd had to do that. Afterwards she kicked my dad out, but he was back and forth a lot. It took about a year for him to finally leave. Now he lives about five minutes away from us.

"We used to hear the fights—our house isn't that big. My dad would be drunk a lot, especially on weekends, and my mom would say something he didn't like and he'd get mad and then they'd be fighting. They got pretty physical. My mom isn't weak and she can fight. She'd throw stuff at him—one time she hit him in the head with an iron. Lots of times my older brother would get between them and try to make them stop.

"There were other times when my mom called the cops. Sometimes my dad would rough us kids up and the cops would knock on the door and then they'd go away when everything got quiet."

Eduardo's parents were young when they met and they're still tied together emotionally, even though they've been divorced for several years. Eduardo tries hard to understand their bond and to explain it to me.

"My mom was fourteen when they met. Dad's two or three years older. Even after all they've been through, I think my mom's torn

inside. She says they'll never get back together, and I believe her, even though she doesn't go out with other guys. But I was surprised at first when she told me she still loves him, that he was the only person she ever really loved, that she'll always love him.

"She talks to us about Dad but she doesn't put him down. She tells us not to let their relationship affect the way we feel about him."

There was a time when Eduardo's mom considered taking her husband back, despite what she had heard about his relationships with other women, despite the drunken abuse, despite the fighting that the kids could always hear.

"It almost happened one Christmas a few years after she threw him out. For a long time she'd heard from her friends that he had a lot of girlfriends, but this one time he told her he didn't have anyone else and that he really wanted to try again with her. But one night she drove past his house and saw the car of one of her girlfriends parked out front, and that did it.

"She came back home and got the baseball bat she'd given to one of my brothers for Christmas and went to my dad's house and smashed the car. After that she cut all ties with her old friend and I think that's when she decided my dad was never going to change.

"I think my dad has regrets. He tells Mom she's the only one he's ever really loved and that he misses us," Eduardo says.

He tries to explain the problems both parents had before they even met, and how those influenced the way they handled marriage and family.

"I know my parents didn't have easy lives when they were young. My grandparents were real mean to my dad, forced him to go to work early and to pay rent. He left home when he was seventeen. My mom is the youngest in her family by about twelve to fourteen years and she essentially grew up as an only child. Her parents died when she was fairly young. So in a way they were looking for family or something when they met."

Eduardo paints a picture of a dad who now, at forty, is still big, exciting, charming—and loaded with bad habits. He sounds like a popular high school jock who's just never been able to grow up.

"He can't be held down. He's fun, strong, and very smart, so smart that he always finds a way to get himself out of trouble. He always seems to have a new girlfriend and seems to like one night flings on the weekends. He drinks a lot but I don't know if he's an alcoholic. I do know he has a pretty big beer belly now."

But the qualities that make Eduardo's father a fun guy at a bar and a magnet for women aren't ones that mesh very well with family life. Eduardo criticizes him for the way he treated his mother.

"I think my mom could really have been hurt in the fighting. My dad used to always put

her down, tell her things that would make her feel bad about herself, and for a long time she believed him. She's the victim."

After the official divorce, Eduardo's father didn't come around to the house very much, which suited the family just fine, he says.

"He was a real deadbeat, defaulted on the custody payments and never went to court. He didn't come around for the first few years and that was okay with us because we were all mad at him. I was really mad at first and I had to try to get used to it. I realized he'll always have some girl and that he's not going to change for us."

Like so many other teenagers, Eduardo didn't discuss the divorce with friends or even with his brothers and sisters when it happened. But even though he still has a hard time opening up, he doesn't advocate silence.

"It's just the way I am. I don't ever have anything big to talk about. I don't tell my mom most things. And I didn't talk about it with my brothers and sisters. We're not really close and we don't talk about many things in general. I don't think we're emotionally disturbed, though, or that the divorce affected us that much.

"My older brother always looked out for himself. We're not a physically affectionate family. This," Eduardo says, *holding up his*

clenched fists, "is the only physical affection we show each other.

"But I'm not saying that's the best way to handle things. I think it's a good idea to let someone know what's going on and to go to someone you trust for advice.

"I'm still mad at my dad for what he did, although I've never told him that. I've never really been able to talk to him, because I never know how he'll react to anything I say. But I wish the divorce hadn't happened, that I hadn't been subjected to all the fighting, that I didn't have to see what it did to my mother."

Eduardo has found some positive ways to channel his disappointment, hurt, and frustration. He had a friend who went away to a private school and Eduardo knew he was smarter than he was, so on his own, he researched schools and scholarships and found a way to go to an out-of-state boarding school. Being away, he says, has helped him gain some perspective.

He's also decided not to let his family situation keep him down. He's looking ahead to careers and thinks now he might want to be a real estate or corporate lawyer. He believes he'll marry someday, but he's not going to do things the same way as his parents.

"For one thing, I won't marry young, like they did. I think early to mid-thirties is best. I'll make sure I know the person well. And once I get married, I won't fool around. I won't ever hit my wife or my kids. I'll let them know if

things are wrong or if I'm upset, but I will never resort to violence.

"I won't make my wife feel bad about her-self. I think my mom has gotten over the nega-tive stuff my dad told her about herself, but she believed it for too long a time."

Eduardo's in a divorce support group at school, and he's found that to be a safe place where he can talk about his life with other kids who can understand how he feels. But he still has the idea that he has to keep up an iron front. He still feels that the messy family details should be kept private.

"My advice to kids going through divorce is to stay strong. Don't let it bother you. I tried hard to keep my mind off it and I didn't let anybody know how I was feeling. I didn't want anyone to know what was happening because I wanted to protect my family."

Violence has been a big part of Eduardo's experi-ence. When he tells me how he'll never resort to it when he gets married, I suspect he feels confused about whether it's ever an appropriate way to deal with prob-lems. He's certainly had his share of black nights with police knocking at the door.

"I tried to stop my dad a few times, and my brother did too, especially when Dad would go after us kids. You know, when it comes down to fighting, I don't think the best thing is for

kids to just lay in bed and shake. Call the cops. That stopped it a few times in my family.''

Even though he's a smart kid who's trying to learn from his family's problems, Eduardo's still stumped about how things got so bad and why no one was able to turn things around.

''I wish things could have been handled differently, but I don't really know how they could have. Nobody ever wanted to talk about it.''

CHAPTER ELEVEN

SUMMING UP AND LOOKING TO THE FUTURE

When I listen again to the tape recordings of my conversations with the kids and adults you've met in this book, I can see a puzzle very clearly. It's this: most of the kids say their biggest problem is their inability to talk with family and friends about how their parents' divorce affected them. But psychologists and counselors and lawyers who work with kids say one way of coming to terms with what's happening is to do just that: talk it out.

The professionals I spoke with agree that it's very difficult for adolescents to understand and overcome on their own the problems of divorce. They're too young and there's too much rejection, too little help from parents caught in their own misery, and too few people outside the family able or willing to help.

Kids also know they can't do it on their own, but they can't see anyone coming to the rescue, either. So lots of them assume a ''suck it up and get on with it'' approach and pretend life isn't falling apart. But that's about as effective as putting a Band-Aid on a broken leg. The injury won't heal properly, and the pain's likely to linger and get worse.

So you're in the process of witnessing your parents' divorce, or you've been living with it for a few years now. What do you do? Listen again to what the kids are trying to tell you:

TRY TO FIND A DIVORCE SUPPORT GROUP

Without exception, the kids I talked with who were part of support groups found them good places to share feelings and to learn from experiences of other kids. They could risk exposing their feelings and feel fairly sure that they wouldn't be shocking anybody. They could listen to how others who had gone before them handled situations they were wrestling with now.

Look for divorce support groups in your school, church, or maybe a social service agency in your community. If there isn't anything like this in your school, ask a guidance counselor to consider starting one. Try to get over being reticent about asking; a group like this can do a great deal to help you handle your anger and pain.

CONFIDE IN YOUR
BROTHERS AND SISTERS

You may have grown up squabbling with them, but you all need each other when your parents are getting divorced. It's important to share memories and feelings, to compare reactions, and to become allies in a difficult time. You'll always be related no matter what happens, and good relationships will be a source of comfort in the years ahead.

TURN TO YOUR EXTENDED FAMILY

American families are spread all over the country these days, which often makes it difficult to develop close relationships with relatives. But think about aunts and uncles, grandparents, even cousins who would be good people to talk with. They know your family, they may have insights into what's been going on, and they might be able to help you understand how to move forward.

LOOK FOR A FRIEND TO TALK TO

Maybe you have a close friend you can confide in. Even if your friend isn't also from a divorced family, if it's the kind of person who can listen, you'll feel better just being able to confide your feelings.

SEARCH FOR ADULTS WHO CAN HELP

How about a school counselor? They're trained to help kids in trouble and they won't think you're weird or bad because your parents are getting divorced. Try making an appointment to talk about what's going on and how it might be affecting your school work. That's a good place to start.

Do you have close relationships with the parents of

any of your friends? They probably have an idea of what you're going through and might be able to listen.

What about a church or synagogue? If you're part of a youth group or know your religious leaders, ask them for some help. They may be able to talk with you one-on-one or recommend groups to get involved in.

WRITE ABOUT WHAT'S
GOING ON

Some kids keep a journal or write letters. Those are both good ways of getting your feelings out of your head and heart and down on paper, where you can see them. You may be surprised at what comes out of your pen or computer. But don't be worried if it isn't of Shakespearean quality—just write.

GO OUT FOR A SPORT

Even if you're not a terrific athlete, look for a sport that might hold your interest. Being part of a team will get you out of yourself and into a group. Focusing on doing well and trying to win is a healthy way to channel your anger.

GET INVOLVED IN
ACTIVITIES

Clubs at school will take up your time in the afternoons after school and give you something to think about besides your family. Church youth groups run lots of activities and community organizations often have service projects that are worth looking into. Volunteer at your local hospital or homeless shelter for a few hours a week.

DEVELOP YOUR TALENTS
AND CREATIVITY

We're all creative in some way, and we all have talents. Listen to yourself to discover what yours are, and pursue them. You may be a painter, a dancer, an athlete, a good listener, a good friend. Take the time to develop your own special interests.

WORK OUT THE NEW RELATIONSHIPS
IN YOUR FAMILY

You may not like the fact that your parents have divorced, but that doesn't mean you need to blame one or both of them and cut yourself off from them. You still need both parents, but it may be up to you to try to rearrange things so you can relate to them in new ways. Try to stuff down your anger and accept their invitations to do things with you. Get to know stepparents and stepbrothers and stepsisters, so your life will be enriched with new family members.

PURSUE NEW RELATIONSHIPS

Divorce means the family relationships you've always known will be different, but that doesn't mean there aren't lots of people out there to meet and become friends with. Chances are you've already got friends you've grown up with or gone to school with for a while. Think about expanding your circle by making an effort to get to know new people you think you might enjoy.

GET SOME EXERCISE

Go for a bike ride. Take a walk. Run. Do something physical. Chances are it will make your feel better.

FIND A PLACE OF YOUR OWN

It can be in a local park or in your backyard. Some kids find some peace in a private spot where they can go to think or meditate or read.

THINK ABOUT THE FUTURE

Your parents are getting divorced, not you. You've got your whole life to live, so think about what you want to study, the kind of career you might want to have, the family you'd like to have someday.

PLAN THE KIND OF MARRIAGE
AND FAMILY YOU WANT

Divorce can actually be positive if it makes you think seriously about what marriage and family mean. You know what you haven't liked and what has caused you pain, and you can choose not to make those same mistakes.

All kids suffer from divorce. Even when it's handled well, it's hard for everyone involved. But with help, you can learn to use the pain to make you stronger than you might have been.

"Kids can do well," said David Brewer, who runs divorce support groups for Beach Acres, a private foundation in Cincinnati, Ohio. His organization designs curriculums for support groups and teaches counselors how to run them.

"Kids can grow, they can learn to become independent, and they can learn how to solve problems. They can even increase their self- esteem when they see they can find ways to handle things positively. All of life's experiences become grist for the mill. But kids need help," said Brewer. "They can't do it alone."

FOR FURTHER READING

Bradley, Buff. *Where Do I Belong?* New York: Harper and Row, 1985.

Gardner, Richard. *The Boys and Girls Book About Divorce*. Northvale, N.J.: Aronson, 1992.

Hamm, Diane Johnston. *Second Family*. New York: Macmillan, 1992.

Hazen, Barbara Shook. *Two Homes to Live In: A Child's-Eye View of Divorce*. New York: Human Sciences Press, 1978.

INDEX

ABOUT THE AUTHOR

Nancy O'Keefe Bolick is the corporate communications manager for a small environmental company and is involved in environmental consulting, as well as being a freelance writer. She has taught English in senior and junior high school, and currently she is a part-time instructor of commercial writing for business people. Her previously published books for young adults were on the inventions and villages of the Shakers.

She and her husband live in Massachusetts and have two children, one a teenager and one a young adult.